REFLECTIONS OF LIFE

by

Clark Elliott

W0006440

authorHOUSE®

AuthorHouse™
1663 Liberty Drive, Suite 200
Bloomington, IN 47403
www.authorhouse.com
Phone: 1-800-839-8640

First published by AuthorHouse 7/25/2007

ISBN: 978-1-4343-1943-2 (sc)

Printed in the United States of America
Bloomington, Indiana

This book is printed on acid-free paper.

Poetry has been a part of Clark since childhood. His great sense of humor have evolved into many poems that have won awards. His poem 20 20 won first place in the NFSPS National contest in 2006. He was named Poet Laureate of the Poetry Society of Oklahoma in 2003. Clark also writes more seriously including his love for God and family. We believe you will enjoy this delightful book of poetry.

This book is dedicated to Louise, the light of my life, who has been my number one fan and greatest encourager over the years. Without her love and support this book would not be published.

I also dedicate this book to David, Debbie and Mark, three of the greatest kids in the world and grandchildren Chris and Ashley Meyer Stoner, Jenna and C.J. Elliott.

TABLE OF CONTENTS

SECOND CHILDHOOD

When I'm an old senior, I won't live alone
Or spend all my life in some nursing home,
Three months with each child, heaven forbids
I'll have nothing to do when I live with my kids.

When they're expecting a call, you'll hear a moan
I'm talking to cronies, spending hours on the phone,
Coming in from outdoors I won't wipe my feet
And always be late when they call me to eat.

I won't make up my bed or pick up my room
Leave clothes on the floor and never use a broom,
I'll leave fingerprints on windows, write on the wall
When I am summoned, pretend I don't hear their call.

When I leave the house, I'll forget my door key
And eat snacks on the couch while watching T.V.
"Dad, glad you could come," as they bite their lip
"Your three months are up, it's time for your trip."

It's my time to leave and as I walk out the gate
I hear music and dancing as they celebrate!

THE NOBLE MAN (A TRIOLET)

The Noble Man who makes a noble plan
Is like a stream of water in the desert.
He is like a richly laden caravan
The Noble Man who makes a noble plan.
He has been a leader since time began
Working with others in harmonious concert.
The Noble Man who makes a noble plan
Is like a stream of water in the desert.

MY ARTISTIC MOTHER

You painted no portraits
For the Sistine Chapel of Rome,
Yet you showed us Madonna
As you lived like one at home.

You wrote no literary masterpieces
Or filled museums with priceless art,
But you demonstrated perfection
With your warm and loving heart.

You chiseled no noted statutes
Out of Cararra marble so fine,
Yet you sculpted a living being
When you shaped this heart of mine.

You erected no great monument
With an exquisitely designed facade,
But your whole life was a temple
Wherein dwelt the Living God.

Oh, how I wish I had the gift
For some immortal design,
I would erect an eternal edifice
To the saintly mother of mine.

FROG PRINCE

A witch got a prince in her grip
Now you're a frog was her quip
    A princess agog
    Kissed the old frog
And now she has warts on her lip!

THE LIGHTHOUSE

In sailing the stormy seas of life
I have a lighthouse who is my wife,
And when my channels seem so few
Her steadfast beams guide me through.

Even in life's darkest night
Ever guiding is her light,
She has guided other ships too
Her radiant rays are ever true.

I'm not afraid out on life's dark sea
Knowing my lighthouse waits for me,
And when I reach my final shore
And my time at sea is no more.

What a glorious radiant sight
To see God's brilliant Shekinah light,
On my knees I give thanks and pray
For my lighthouse who lit my way.

HIDDEN TREASURES

I met a country girl in December
Whose shape was rather curvy,
And she had this little walk
That made her hips a little swervy.

I found out in the summertime
Much to my sorrow and despair,
I found those December curves
Was just bunched up underwear.

IRON MAN

When I was a young man
My kids thought I could do it all,
Mending daughter's broken dolls
And teaching the boys to bat a ball.

To have a long and fun vacation
When our schedule was very tight,
They would sleep in the car
While I would drive all night.

I could work the whole day long
And if things were not going right,
I would stay at the office
And work late into the night.

I would run a mile every day
And regularly exercise at the gym,
And even joined a church league
To play basketball with the men.

Now that fifty years have passed
I thought I was looking just fine,
And took mother to the mall
For her weekly shopping time.

As I was waiting for her in a chair
A three year old girl waved her hand,
And smiling at me very sweetly
She asked, "how are you old man?"

With the words the little girl said
I certainly was disgusted,
For I went and looked into the mirror
And found the Iron Man had rusted!

MY MA BELL AWARD

The phone company held a banquet
And I was invited to speak,
They told me I'd get an award
And it would arrive next week.

The prize was for my presentation
And if my poetry reading excels,
I would get a gold lapel pin
And on it would be three bells.

If my reading was only average
The number of bells would be two,
And if I wasn't any good at all
One bell would have to do.

Next week I received my prize
Which made my ego fall,
For on Ma Bell's lapel pin
There were no bells at all.

It only took a week or two
For my ego to return to size,
For I began telling all my friends
I'd won the Poetry No-Bell prize.

AN EAGLE SCREAMS (A TRIOLET)

Did you hear an eagle scream
When the Twin Towers fell,
Victims of an evil regime
Did you hear an eagle scream
At those who would blaspheme
America with a tragic hell.
Did you hear an eagle scream
When the Twin Towers fell?

PATHS

In this troubled world today
There are many paths to take,
Some will lead to happiness
While others bring heartache.

Some paths lead to nowhere
For just around the bend,
We failed to see the warning
That it would abruptly end.

Other paths lead to somewhere
Be careful which you choose,
For at the end of each one
Someone will win or loose.

Getting off the beaten path
Can brings struggle and strife,
As we take that long old journey
That most folks call "our life."

What path have you taken
You must choose it well,
For some lead up to heaven
While others down to hell.

When I depart this earth
And lie beneath the sod,
I pray the path I've taken
Is the one that leads to God.

WAITING

She sits alone in an old nursing home
  Waiting for some friend to call,
With one good ear, she hopes to hear
  Friendly footsteps in the hall.

With legs now lame using her cane
  To hobble to the front door,
Hoping they're late, she sits to wait
  But no one comes any more.

More hair turns grey each passing day
  More pain creeps into her shoulder,
Failing health took all her wealth
  It's hell to keep getting older.

She remembers when many young men
  Wanted her for their bride,
The one that won and gave her a son
  Is now buried on the hillside.

She looks for her son or just anyone
  To come and make a call,
And begins to pray this be the day
  But no one comes at all.

Is there an old friend where you can spend
  Several hours of your day,
Don't leave them in gloom in some dark room
  You'll receive a blessing I pray.

THE FUNNY ZOO

I dreamed I went to the funny zoo
Where the elephant was colored blue,
And the brown bear wasn't brown
He was purple wearing a golden crown..

The kingly lion did not have a mane
And was licking on a candy cane.
The monkey said, "I have to sneeze,
Will you pass the Kleenex please?"

The big old hippo didn't like to swim
He'd rather play volley ball in the gym,
And the striped tiger didn't like to eat meat
A hot fudge sundae was his favorite treat.

The green giraffe who was very tall
Liked to slam dunk the basketball.
Why the rhino, no one really knows
Liked to dance on his tippy toes.

When I visited the polka dotted snake
She was eating her birthday cake.
Sleeping in his bed was the alligator
saying, "can't talk now, I'll see you later.

But the animal with the biggest smile
Was on the face of the crocodile,
While the ostrich was taking a snooze
All dressed up in her red tennis shoes.

The admission to the Funny Zoo is free
Wouldn't you like to come along with me?"

RETURN TO THE FUNNY ZOO

I dreamed I returned to the Funny Zoo
And have exciting things to tell to you,
The ostrich head wasn't in the sand
He was singing in a hard rock band.

The zebra didn't have black and white stripes
He was very green and played Scottish bag pipes.
When I visited the home of the water buffalo
He invited me in to see a new T.V. show.

I found the camel did not have a hump
And was using a rope to hop, skip and jump.
Then I strolled upon a little baby kangaroo
Who couldn't go hopping, he had lost his shoe.

High in an oak tree was the big hairy ape
Playing he was superman, wearing a red cape,
I wandered upon a herd of big horn sheep
Who said, "be quiet, we're trying to sleep."

Next on my stop was the big northern moose
Who was eating pancakes and drinking orange juice.
And there were no stickers on the old porcupine
She was getting a tan in the warm sunshine.

All of the funny zoo animals became my friend
And I can't wait until I go to sleep again.

GROWN UP CHILDREN

Five year old daughter Sally
And her little brother Mose,
Pretended they were grown ups
By wearing grown up clothes.

They went visiting to the neighbors
To make a neighborly call,
"Come in for some lemonade
Don't stand there in the hall."

After several glasses of lemonade
Sally said our visit is through,
We must return to our home
There's something we have to do.

Can't you stay for more lemonade?
"No," Sally said with a sheepish glance,
We must return home at once
My husband just wet his pants!

ROYAL FLUSH

There was a medical doctor
Who was losing nightly slumber,
For his toiled would not flush
So he had to call the plumber.

He called him late at night
Saying my problem is not much,
Except I can't use the bathroom
As my toiled will not flush.

So you're a medical doctor
He said with words not charming,
Throw two aspirins in the commode
And call me in the morning.

COLD WINTERS AND WARM MEMORIES

When winter winds are blowing
And the snow drifts far and wide,
I am filled with warm memories
Of when you laid down by my side.

I think of you in the springtime
And I miss you in the fall,
But when winter winds are blowing
That's when I miss you most of all.

For I am reminded of that time
That occurred long, long ago,
When we walked for many hours
Amidst the softly falling snow.

It was then you said you loved me
Which gave my heart a thrill,
The warmness of your embrace
Shut out the winter's chill.

Our hearts were young and foolish
Making promises we could not keep,
But the memories of that night
Still haunts me in my sleep.

As I look back over the years
That has turned my hair to grey,
The warm memories of that night,
Keep cold winter winds away.

GRANDMA'S APRON

Some Grandmas wore their aprons
To protect their Sunday dress,
My Grandmas was more useful
And she looked quite picturesque.

Grandma used hers to carry eggs
And even clean out my dirty ears,
When I was sad and hurting
It also wiped away my tears.

When the weather turned a little cool
She used it to cover up her arms,
And she brought in baby chicks
That hatched out in the barn.

From the garden in the springtime
The apron carried beans and baby peas,
In the fall it held red apples
That had fallen from the trees.

She daily went to the woodpile
And Grandma never seemed to tire,
Of filling that apron with kindling
To start the early morning fire.

When unexpected company came
The apron quickly wiped away the dust,
And became a potholder for the oven
Removing pies with flaky crust.

When thunder and lightening crashed
With the terror that it brings,
My favorite secret hiding place
Was inside Grandma's apron strings.

A BALLAD
CALLOUSED HANDS

A reporter asked a workman
With toil-worn calloused hands,
just what labor he was doing
To make this building grand.

The workman said, "hands like these shaped
The Coliseum at Rome,
Constructed Paris's Eiffel Tower
And a quaint cottage home.

They hoisted steel into the air
To build the Empire State,
And bridged the deep cold waters at
Francisco's Golden Gate.

In the hills of South Dakota
They hewed presidents' faces,
Raised the Notre Dame Cathedral
With its airy gothic graces.

They formed stately basilicas
In London there's Saint Paul,
In distant lands of India
Is graceful Taj Mahal.

Worn hands worked through the ages with
 Guggenheim's Museum of Art,
And Sydney Harbors' Opera House
Delights any dreamers heart.

Workmen with calloused hands like mine
Gave all they had to give;
Their sweat and labor makes the world
A better place to live."

PEACE

We sing of peace in the valley
The peace of a baby asleep,
And what could be more serene
Than a resting flock of sheep.

There is a restful glow I feel
Watching a sinking sun in the West,
Or hearing the voice of a lark
Winging homeward to her nest.

There is a tranquil peace I feel
Overlooking a valley of farms,
Or hearing the voice of a child
Rocked in it's mothers arms.

There is a peace that comes
When praying on bended knees,
Knowing the power of your God
Is greater than any disease.

Facing all the problems of life
The greatest peace I've come to know,
Is the breaking of Easter flowers
Through the last of Winter's snow.

TRUE LOVE

She brought her new friend home
To met her Mother and Dad,
They hoped it wasn't serious
That this was just another fad.

For they didn't like the tattoos
That ran up and down the arm,
And the surly arrogance
Added nothing to the charm.

The Levi's were cut too low
They barely hung on the hips,
Two rings were in the earlobe
A cigarette dangled from the lips.

The hair stood up in spikes
And was dyed a brilliant red,
If this friendship is permanent
There is something here to dread.

Rings in the nose and eyebrows
Gave little cause for joy,
They hoped daughter's next friend
Not be a girl but a boy.

OLD POETS AND WARM MEMORIES

When my soul is sad and troubled
    What brings relief to this heart of mine,
Is reading an old volume of poetry
    With thoughts in prose and rhyme.

I like to read the lesser known poets
    Some write of a long lost love,
Now lying beneath the sod
    But their soul is with God above.

They write of the song of the lark
    And roses all covered with dew,
Of childhood days in the country
    And old friends so loyal and true.

The tell of fields, forests and flowers
    And three crosses on a far away hill,
Of wars, battles and lost loved ones
    Warming my heart from winter's chill.

There are poems of passing seasons
    Of spring, winter, summer and fall,
But the poetry about dear Mothers
    Are the ones I love most of all.

.When I am finished reading the poems
    And my burdened soul is set free,
I thank God for all of his poets
    For they're always a blessing to me!

GRANDMA NELL

Come my friend and sit for a spell
There is a story I'd like to tell
Of a city girl who left her home
As her husband wanted to roam
This is the adventures of Grandma Nell.

They sold their house to make a trip
To get in line at the Cherokee Strip;
There was land to be had for free
That once belonged to the Cherokee,
A home in the Panhandle was their destiny.

Grandma drove that wagon for several days
Beneath the sun's hot scorching rays.
Grandma Nell drove that wagon team
Right across a deep swift moving stream,
To stake their claim without any delay.

She helped dig up large earthen clods
To build a dugout out of the sod,
To face winter blizzards, cold and cruel
With only Buffalo chips to use for fuel;
What kept her going was faith in God.

There were many days she was left alone
And all of her babies were born at home.
Drinking water came from a nearby creek
And many days the future looked bleak;
Pioneer living is not for the weak..

During rain storms the sod roof would leak
And muddy drops fell on her cheek.
The sod home could be quite cold and damp
Or as hot and dusty as a coal miner's camp,
With the only light was from a coal oil lamp.(cont.)

22

Years of poverty gnawed at her pride
With two tiny crosses on the hillside;
Yet over the years she made no complaint
Living the life of an unsung saint
Who never allowed their dream to grow faint.

Oh, Pioneer Grandmother, strong and true
Holding family together, you were the glue.
As I stand proudly over your small grave
I thank you for the life you so valiantly gave
And all other pioneer mothers just as brave.

I'M WISHING

Sam, the King of Assyria was low on cash
Fighting the Hittites took most of his stash,
His last possession was the Euphrates Star
The most valuable diamond in the world by far.
He took it to a pawnbroker to get a loan
The offer of a thousand dinars made him groan.
I paid ten thousand dinars for that said King Sam
I am the King, don't you know who I am?
The Broker replied, "when you wish to pawn a star
It makes no difference who you are."

ANNUAL CRITTER'S PARADE

Odd creatures from across the land
Formed the Critters marching band,
Leading the parade was the Orangaton
Whirling and twirling a golden baton.

Then came a Wunky looking sad and glum
Keeping a beat on his tin can drum.
Marching proudly was the Unicorn
Blowing loudly on a Pantuba horn.

The Watamapotamus I've never met
Was cleverly playing a clarinet,
And a good musician is the Armidello
As she strummed on her blue chello.

A pink Tigalow looked quite cute
Blowing hard on a wingding flute.
A baby Wossum who was very liddle
Kept in step with a one string fiddle.

A Giraffalo right from Noah's Ark
Was strumming on a five string harp,
But the Mooskie had to march alone
He couldn't play the clairaphone.

The Liger showed he was very nimble
Banging and clashing his red hot cymbal.
The parade was a real lollapalozza
Playing marches by John Phillips Sousa.

This is the story that I wanted to hear
Odd critters band meets once a year,
And no one can ever dissuade
Me from attending next year's parade.

ECHOES IN MY HEART

When I stroll alone in the evening dew
Echoing in my heart are thoughts of you,
Of how in the Spring under budding trees
You gave my hand an extra squeeze
And promised you would be eternally mine
And I would forever be, your valentine.

Thoughts come of holding sunburned hands
As we walked in the tide over glistening sands,
Thoughts come of that hot summers day
When we walked in fields of fresh mown hay,
And how we strolled under Autumn's trees
Frolicking and dancing among golden leaves.

Of sitting by the fireside at winter time
And sipping a glass of strawberry wine.
I think of days and nights that used to be
That are forever enshrined in my memory,
But just hearing echoes won't have to do
Although I still have them, I still have you.

ENGLISH SPOKEN HERE

I remember my old English Teacher
Saying "dearest little student creature,
You know using bad English is a curse
Be sure to write with proper verse."

The rules are quite definitive
It is wrong to split an infinitive,
Another of her astute observations
Always avoid annoying alliterations.

Your writing will never be terrific
If you are just more or less specific,
And another thing you must memorize
One should never generalize.

To make sure your readers are never bored
The passive voice must be ignored,
And what gives readers indigestion
Is asking them a rhetorical question.

If our writing is to be superb
Never use an adjective for a verb,
And what causes a billion consternations
Is using too many wild exaggerations.

A comparison is as bad as a cliche
And we don't use them at all today,
And here's another proven angle
Don't let your participles dangle.

Apostrophes can show possession
And proper use is not in question,
Using good English is always fun
When you avoid the unnecessary pun.(cont.)

Don't become like the local yokel
Using phrases that are colloquial,
Praises to teacher I shout and holler
For making me an English scholar.

20 20

When she awoke this morning
Her face would stop a clock,
So she made an appointment
To see her family medical Doc.

Saying, "when I looked in the mirror
My hair was rather frizzy,
Both eyes were kind of bloodshot
And I looked a little dizzy.

There were wrinkles on my cheeks
And furrows lined my brow,
A wart was on my nose
That's why I'm seeing you now.

What's wrong with me Doctor"
She said with heavy sighs,
He said, "I don't know lady
But it's certainly not your eyes.

THE PINK DRESS

As I come home from work each day
I see a sad young girl sitting alone,
The passerbys just walk on past her
As if she was a tainted ugly crone.

Always wearing a wrinkled pink dress
While her feet are soiled and bare,
Yet no one even stops to look at her
And no one really seems to care.

I decided the next day to make a visit
And approached her sitting there,
Thinking she shouldn't be left alone
With so many strangers everywhere.

When I came much closer to her
I could see her back was deformed,
Under the dress was a huge hump
I wished I had the power to transform.

When I sat down and smiled at her
She shyly returned my smile,
We talked on until it was evening
I was glad I went that extra mile.

I asked her why she looked so sad
And she said, "I am different from you,"
I said, "you look just like an angel
And as pure as the morning dew.

I think you are like a Guardian Angel
Sent to watch over those passing by,"
She said, " you have guessed correctly
And now Im going to show you why."(cont.)

She opened the back of the pink dress
And unfurled her angelic wings,
I stared on in amazement
Privileged to see these hallowed things.

She said," finally you have thought
Of some one other than just you,
My job here on earth is finished
I am glad we had this rendezvous."

I asked why no other people helped her
She said "you're the only one who can see me."
With a sweep of her wings she was gone
But she changed my life completely.

SNOWFLAKE

Snowflake, snowflake
Falling to earth,
Who gave to you
Miraculous birth.

Snowflake, snowflake
Caressing my cheek,
As Heaven's creation
You're truly unique.

We too are unique
As God's creation,
Sing songs of praise
In celebration!

SPRING IN MY HEART

It's always spring in my heart
With the first song of the lark,
Who pushes away winter's gloom
Bringing joy to my lonely room.

Then comes sultry days of June
When all of nature is in tune,
A word to summer, I impart
It's always spring in my heart.

Autumn will come again this year
Yet, I'll not shed a single tear,
It's time for the colors of fall to start
But it's always spring in my heart.

When I feel the cold winds blow
And see the flakes of winter's snow,
I know these things will soon depart
For it's always spring in my heart.

BIG BANG

This universe came from dust
And is called The Big Bang Theory,
But this dust came out of nowhere
Of this theory, I'm rather leery.

What the Bible said on creation
Is still good enough for me,
I think the beginning started
When God said, "let there be!"

HOW IT ENDS

One golden daybreak without warning
 the blazoned sky rolled up like a scroll of parchment
while a blood red moon dangles in the sky.
Planets and galaxies recede beyond the threshold
of infinity. The shuddering earth propels
the seismographs off the Richter Scale
as skyscrapers topple like a row of dominos.
The seas, a maelstrom of tsunami waves,
engulf the costal lands and islands, annihilating
all in it's mad surge to cataclysmic destruction.
Fire plummets to a land tinder dry from drought
creating a smoldering wasteland.
Oh, yes, we were continually warned;
the birth pangs of the end begins.

THAT FACE (MINUTE POEM)

Returning from the art gallery
your face I see.
Always haunting
ever taunting
bringing visions to my tired mind,
why be unkind?
You know my love
is from above.
Mona Lisa please have a heart
though we're apart
you still beguile
with your sad smile.

GALL BLADDER BLUES

I spoke with Doctor Bell
Who said, "there's not a doubt,
Your gall bladders full of stones
And that sucker must come out."

The hospital had a procedure
They say it worked real fine,
I was placed on a conveyer belt
And a surgical assembly line.

They put a needle in my arm
At least that's what I was told,
But I don't remember anything
For I was knocked out cold.

My stomach was filled with gas
So everyone could see,
Where to put the instruments
For my bladder was on T.V.

A clamp here and a snip there
My bladder was separated,
It was on the T.V. again
And wasn't even rated.

Dr. Bell said my past pain
Came from eating like a glutton,
And he drug out that old bladder
Right through my belly button.

A stitch here and a suture there
Now my tummy's in full bloom,
And I was back on the conveyor belt
To wake up in the recovery room.(cont.)

When they checked my insurance
And saw the benefits were small,
They said, "hurry, get dressed
You can't stay here at all."

And to make my day even worse
Here's what my wife had to say,
"The TLC that I'm giving you
Is only good for one more day!"

BLOWING IN THE WIND

Out on a barren homestead
A shattered windmill stands,
Once a proud piece of machinery
Erected by an early settlers hand.

Most of the blades are gone now
Falling to winds and red dust,
While the iron shaft to the well
Is being eroded away by rust.

It once brought forth fresh water
To nurture man and flock,
But the homestead and the mill
Fell to time's relentless clock.

Like me, it once stood proudly
To be of service to mankind;
From many years of toil and labor
We've fallen to the sands of time.

MAGIC LAND

To see the beauty of America
Please plan a trip today,
For the scenery of Oklahoma
Will take your breath away.

Kiamicha has wilderness trails
And take Talimena's scenic drive,
Watching the sun set on the Salt Plains
Makes you glad that you're alive.

Wade the bubbly springs of Sulphur
And climb Red Rock Canyon walls,
Gaze on Waynokas shifting sand dunes
And the majesty of Turner Falls.

See the famed Azelias at Muskogee;
Oil derricks on Capitols' ground,
Tour historic old Black Mesa
Where dinosaur bones are found.

Drive along historic Route Sixty Six
And walk on the trail of tears,
See how Indians lived in tepees
When cowboys herded steers.

Wichita Mountains Wildlife Refuge
Has a herd of shaggy buffalo,
Yes, the beauty of our landscape
Will set any soul aglow.

MOTHER'S HANDS

I remember as a little child
Those work worn hands of mother,
That brushed the tears away
Of me and little brother.

They were not white or small
But filled with toil worn lines,
From years of daily work
As if sculpted by one Divine.

Those hands kept toiling on
With chores day after day,
There was no time for leisure
There was no time for play.

The laundry must be done
And there was meals to prepare;
Torn clothes to be mended
But always time for prayer.

The garden must be planted
If there will be food to eat,
And the weeds must be hoed
Despite the summers' heat.

I paid so little attention
As those hands grew old and worn,
How time had left it's mark
From the labor they had borne.

For that fateful day arrived
When Mother was laid to rest,
And those dear old wrinkled hands
Were folded across her breast. (cont.)

I know a day is coming where
I'll step into the promised lands,
And hold again my Mothers'
Precious wrinkled hands.

WINTER EVENING (A VILLANELLE)

The sinking sun has lost it's amber glow
as winter's hush comes tumbling down the hill;
so quietly do the dark woods fill with snow.

I do not understand nature, although
the constant change of seasons bring a thrill;
the sinking sun has lost it's amber glow.

I see nature in the soft winds that blow
laying a blanket on each rock and rill;
so quietly do the dark woods fill with snow.

As the deep purple night draws on, I grow
strangely warm in spite of winter's chill;
the sinking sun has lost it's amber glow.

The downy flakes descend to earth below
and cover the once blooming daffodil,
so quietly do the dark woods fill with snow.

When I watch God in his workings, I know
a deeper love for Him they will instill;
the sinking sun has lost it's amber glow,
so quietly do the dark woods fill with snow.

LORETTO CHAPEL MIRACLE

The Sisters Chapel was complete
The Nuns caught unaware,
There was no way to the choir loft
Some one left out the stair.

They sought the counsel of craftsmen
Their reports added gloom;
They said a stair could not be built
The builders left no room.

The Sisters made a Novena
Their faith was never faint,
They lifted prayers to Saint Joseph;
Carpenter's patron Saint.

When the Novena days were over
Some said it was a quirk,
An unknown carpenter showed up
And said, "I need some work."

The carpenter used wooden pegs
The wire nails he refused,
Holding thirty three steps as one
The loft could now be used.

A time of labor came and went
The stair was complete,
Two flawless spirals rising up;
Oh, what a builders feat!

When the sisters sought the worker
To pay his salary,
They found he'd vanished in the night
And left a mystery. (cont.)

Legend says it was Saint Joseph
Who answered the Nuns prayers,
He came in flesh to Santa Fe
To build those splendid stairs.

OLD TRAILS

Where have all the trails gone
That used to cover our land,
Blazed by grizzled settlers
Or nomadic Indian bands.

These old trails are vanishing
Both the Indian and Pioneer,
Those carved out by brave men
In search of a new frontier.

Some rimmed the edge of canyons
Others followed a valley stream,
One went west to Oregon
Where each one chased a dream.

Others went deep into the forests
Each trail was marked with care,
To lead to the hunting grounds
For food and clothes to wear.

Some went out west to Abilene
Others Southwest to Santa Fe,
Where cowboys herded the dogies
To make sure they didn't stray.

Some tribes came South for winter
By the shores of lakes they're found,
Some lived by the bow and arrow
While others tilled the ground.

Those trails were the first highways
But they are hard to find now,
Because they're covered with concrete
Or gave way to the farmers plow.(cont.)

Spring will come then winter's snow
That covers the trails, now rare,
Where are the trails of yesteryear
No one seems to know or care.

The only trails we see today
Are made by jets high in the sky,
Lord, let me walk an old trail
Once more before I die.

JUSTICE

Two Doctors and a H.M.O. Manager
All died at the very same time,
When they appeared before St. Peter
He said, "you'll have to get in line."

St. Peter approached the children's doctor
saying, "Where in the world have you been,
You saved a lot of children's lives
Please open the door and come right in."

Then he spoke to the old psychiatrist
"Doctor, you too have eternal life,
You've helped many with their problems
Amid this world's turmoil and strife."

He turned to the H.M.O. Manager
"What good in this world did you do?"
Why I've saved hospitals lots of dollars
And patients unpaid bills I did pursue.

St. Peter said to the HMO manager
"Now hear me and hear me well,
You can come in for just three days
Then you can go to hell!"

THE RICHES OF PINCHING PENNIES

He didn't earn much money
But with the help of God above,
Two could live as cheap as one
And they would live on love.

When Wednesday's paper comes
Many coupons she would clip,
And when it came to fresh meat
That's the aisle they'd skip.

For they couldn't afford any steaks
Or even a hunk of Honey Ham,
But when they used a little ketchup
How delicious was the Spam!

In winter the furnace was turned low
Being cold would not bring harm,
They'd wear a coat inside the house
And that would keep them warm.

There would be no air conditioning
They would brave the summer heat,
And by turning on the window fan
Would bring several hours of sleep.

They couldn't afford new clothes
For the clothing budget was small,
But Goodwill and Salvation Army
Was their favorite shopping mall.

No money to attend the movies
But their entertainment was free,
When they adjusted the rabbit ears
On their old black and white T.V.(cont.)

They only had one automobile
But it caused a lot of smiles,
For it was over 30 years of age
And had over 500 thousand miles.

They didn't have much education
And certainly were not scholars,
 But when they upped and died
They left a million dollars!

RADIANCE (A CINQUAIN)

Moonlight
Reflecting love
In the eyes of lovers
Walking silently with each heart
Aglow

OCTOBER (A CINQUAIN)

Sunlight
On golden leaves
Fluttering in the breeze
Dancing to the music of death
Darkness

THE BEAR FACTS

Once I went hunting for a Polar Bear
There must be one "somewhere out there,"
A Polar Bear trophy was my goal
So I drove my sled to the old North Pole.

After unloading all my hunting gear
I saw Polar Bears both far and near,
I fired my gun until I was almost deaf
And now I had only one shell left.

I sat on a snow bank to eat my lunch
And when it moved I had a hunch,
That I'd better get far away from there
For I had sat down on a sleeping bear.

When he stood up it seems I recall
That old bear was over ten feet tall,
My last bullet didn't have any lead
I'd better think fast or I am dead!

A cold sweat broke out on my brow
Listen carefully to what I tell you now,
I wiped off the sweat for it had froze
And frozen B.B.s rolled off my nose.

I will get you now bear, I did yell
Putting frozen B.B.s in my empty shell,
Raising my gun I took careful aim
What happened next brought me fame.

Heat from the firing made the B.B.s melt
And I can't tell you how terrible I felt,
The explosion made the gun barrel hotter
Those frozen B.B.s became a stream of water.(cont.)

When that stream of water hit the frigid air
Like a frozen spear it flew right at that bear,
And much to my delight and surprise
It hit that old bear right between the eyes.

The bear's warm body caused the ice to melt
But my goal was to get the old bear's pelt,
That Polar Bear died but he didn't feel pain
The cause of his death was water on the brain.

IN ARLINGTON CEMETERY (A RONDEAU)

In Arlington Cemetery, side by side
Lay brother Marines who valiantly died.
One was shot by a sniper in the back
As he and comrades liberated Iraq;
Yet between their graves is a great divide.

At the loss of one life our Nation cried
In his sacrifice we were filled with pride,
Giving up his life in that sneak attack;
In Arlington Cemetery.

The other Marines' death I must confide
His fighting in Viet Nam some did deride.
He did not volunteer for his bivouac
And received no honors when he came back;
Can we lay our discrimination aside
In Arlington Cemetery?

FOR BETTER - FOR WORSE

A new girl arrived at school
He waited 'til she was alone,
Then he introduced himself
Asking, "may I walk you home?"

They were dearest friends for years
Until he knelt on bended knee,
Placing a ring on her finger
"Will you spend your life with me?"

At their whitewashed country church
There he took her to be his wife,
Promising to always love her
As long as she had breath and life.

With not much formal education
He became another working man,
One more in a sea of millions
Who provide the very best they can.

A dreadful disease came to her
Now nothing will be the same,
The doctor said it won't be long
She will not even know her name.

He tenderly cared for her needs
So lovingly every day,
Until that fateful moment came
Where she silently slipped away.

A few came to the grave side
And heard the muffled sound,
As they lowered a wooden casket
Six feet into the ground. (cont.)

Those years of constant care
Took a heavy toll on his health,
And the mounting medical bills
Took what little he had of wealth.

While some would have given up
And others would whine and curse,
He just smiles and said his vows
Was for better or for worse.

DANCING DAISIES

When early springtime comes
They always put on a show,
Poking their yellow heads
Through the crusted snow.

I saw the daisies dancing
How they sway and bend,
Standing rather defiantly
In the brisk March wind.

They know their time is short
Soon their beauty will wane,
Some plucked by young ladies
Just to make a daisy chain.

But when they bowed to me
This sounds a little crazy,
I did a little two step
And became a dancing daisy!

I'M JUST MATURE

That dreaded time in life has come
When the only thing that brings a thrill,
Is to know my prune juice is working
Now that I'm sixty and over the hill.

My knees hurt when I bend over
And I'm getting a little hard to hear,
My hair is getting grey and thinning
And arthritis is creeping in, I fear.

I turn off the lights for economic reasons
But what really leaves me broken hearted,
When I sit down in my rocking chair
I can't get that darn thing started.

I have false teeth and can't remember
And suffer from indigestion,
When it comes to driving at night
That's certainly out of the question.

I have tooth decay and chest pains
Acid reflux and fluid retention,
My stomach is bloated with gas
And makes noises I cannot mention.

I have trouble sleeping and creaky bones
A bell's ringing in my left ear,
A pain is moving down my back
And my thinking is none to clear.

I have halitosis and scoliosis
And other things they cannot cure,
But I'm not really getting older
I am just feeling rather mature.

WERE YOU

Will you be remembered after you're gone
As a person with style and grace,
Who was kind, generous and warm
With a constant smile upon your face?

Were you the one who always sent cards
To your sick and ailing friends,
And if a friend made a mistake
Were you the first to make amends?

When others have treated you unfairly
Were you willing to forgive with a smile,
Did you visit the ill at the hospital;
Were you willing to go that extra mile?

Are you the first to give congratulations
To someone who has found success,
And never interrupt who's talking
Or a sick friend ask God to bless?

Do you open doors for the elderly
And never push to the front of the line,
And when meeting your friends for lunch
Always make sure you're there on time?

There are many ways to compliment
By sending flowers, cards of a gift,
To a friend who's feeling quite low
Do you give their sagging hearts a lift?

Sometimes giving a warm and cheery hello
Is the very thing that someone needs,
And you will forever be remembered
As the friend who did good deeds!

MY CHRISTMAS WISH FOR YOU

I wish I had the magical power
To give these Christmas gifts to you,
One would be a package of happiness
To last the whole year through.

And to help in your success
I would add a wealth of love,
And decorate your soul with joy
Like the kind from up above.

I would tie up in red ribbons
A blessing of good health,
And appreciation from your family
Is all you need of wealth.

I would add a string of smiles
To brighten each and every day,
And have every prayer answered
When upon your knees you pray.

I would take away your heartaches
And every ache and pain you feel,
I would wipe away your tears
And make every dream be real.

I would fill each day with gladness
And add a star to your crown,
To be cast before your Maker
As I know you're Heaven bound!

UNSUNG SAINTS

Mothers, your children look to you
With eyes so innocent and wide,
They put their faith and trust in you;
God has sent you to be their guide.

You teach them how to pray at meals
And put bandages on their knee,
You teach them how to play together
And live in peaceful harmony.

You send them off to kindergarten
While the years go racing past,
You ask on bowed knees in prayer
Lord, why do they grow up so fast?

The time will come to leave the nest
As they will boldly try their wings,
And when they thank you for your care
How your heart within you sings!

Soon they will return home again
For you to meet their husband or wife,
And then your role will start anew
As they bring forth new life.

As Grandmother your start over again
By teaching them right from wrong,
You help them learn the alphabet
And make sure their faith is strong.

When you're called home to heaven
Your children will rise and call you blest,
And they will thank God for Mother
Who taught how to meet life's test.

MY SECRET LIFE

I have been living a secret life
That no one really knows about,
If they heard of my accomplishments
I'm sure there would be some doubt.

When I took mother to the mall
I waited quietly on a bench,
And was approached by two muggers
Thinking I would be a cinch.

I knocked one mugger to the floor
With a deadly karate blow,
While the other dropped to his knees
Begging, please mister let me go.

I went to get some spending money
And went inside the local bank,
When walked in three masked bandits
Whose guns were on me, point blank.

I grabbed the gun from one robber
And filled him full of lead,
When the others saw my sneer
Right out the door they fled.

As I drove along the highway
There was furniture on the curbing
A poor widow was being evicted
I thought this is real disturbing.

I seized that greedy landlord
And forced him to his knees,
Until he begged the widow
"Stay, oh stay will you please."(cont.)

Now don't ask me about my heroics
I think enough already been said,
For I found that I was dreaming
When I woke up lying in my bed.

REVENGE

From the ends of the earth
To the expanse of outer spaces,
Ours are the Grandchildren
With sweet angelic faces.

In their formative years
We have helped them grow,
And in shaping their lives
There's something you should know.

All of their parents rules
Were quickly forgotten,
Instead of strict discipline
We simply spoiled them rotten.

After visiting the darlings
Their orneriness we condoned,
We ruined their parents instruction
Then slipped quietly back to home.

RETURNING

I returned to the old home place I left fifty years ago,
The legs that used to scamper now walk painfully and slow.
Stopped by the old home place once so warm and cheery
The windows were all broken looking so drab and dreary.

I walked out to the barn, the loft once stacked with hay
It was about to fall over and looked in disarray.
I strolled down to Main street and visited the grocery story
Where pickles once soaked in barrels with sawdust on the floor.

I remembered the old blacksmith shop whose forge was red hot,
Now there's just trash and weeds covering a vacant lot.
Drove down to the old creek that once seemed deep and wide
But it only took a little skip to reach the other side.

I came upon the "swimmin hole" where I learned to swim
We boys went "skinnydipping," hung our overalls on a limb.
The water in the "swimmin hole" was never fit to drink,
And it is so much smaller now, wonder what caused it to shrink.

I went to the old school house with three classes in each room,
Smelling the old chalk dust once more to me was sweet perfume.
Seeing the old church still standing with it's whitewashed steeple
Brought fond memories of the past, how I loved those dear people.

Should I have ever returned is the though that comes to me,
Did I tarnish a precious treasure locked in my childhood memory.

A GUARDIAN DAISY

At the Veterans Cemetery
Where lay a soldier brave,
There was a single daisy
A'growing on his grave.

I asked the little daisy
Do you have a story to tell,
The little daisy replied
I do and hear me well.

I am growing here alone
Bringing a message to this youth,
Although he's sleeping now
There is an eternal truth.

I bloom in early springtime
And bask in sunsets glow,
I've faded in the autumn
And slept under winter's snow.

But I rise again each spring
And stretch my petals to the sky,
To show him we can live again
Though the body seems to die.

I am telling my young friend
His soul has gone above,
And he did not die in vain
Thanks to Gods' eternal love.

PIRATES

The dipping sun was blood red
Ending the soft dying day,
The moon comes white and ghostly
While the Pirate ship looks for prey.

Their frigate plies the warm salt water;
Sails catching the warm westerly flow,
And they find repose in secluded coves
That only fugitive pirates know.

With high black boots and cutlass near
And the Jolly Roger furled overhead,
The Captain prowls for treasure ships
And to take their crew alive or dead.

From the Barbary Coast to Portobelo
Any merchant ship will be fair game,
For the goal of cutthroat pirates
Is to murder, loot and maim.

They celebrate their evil plundering
By getting drunk on demon rum,
They will even kill fellow shipmates
Over some bauble they think's a plum.

There are old maps of buried booty
Hidden at the foot of a blazoned tree,
Just outside the surging tide, but
Inside a warm and sheltered lee.

The days of pirating are gone now
And to sail the sea is a pleasure,
Although I wouldn't want to be a pirate
I'd like to find their buried treasure!

I WONDER

Lord, how I've often wondered
Why the righteous suffer most,
And the wicked seem to prosper
Of their riches they do boast.

Is it true that the darkest sinner
No matter how deep he's lost,
Can repent and be redeemed
Because Christ has paid the cost?

I seem to grope alone in darkness
Not knowing which way to go,
Though I daily read your word
There are truths I cannot know.

I now see through a glass darkly
Wondering if the things to come,
Will be so glorious and perfect
That leaves me dazed and numb.

Could I pierce the veil of heaven
That's beyond the endless sky,
And the glories that I see there
Would I want to say goodby.

THIRSTY

Dad went through the nightly ritual
Of tucking his daughter into bed,
As he started to read the paper
Here's what the little girl said.

"Dad, will you go into the kitchen
And please go to the sink,
Just get me a glass of water
For I would like another drink."

Dad said to his little daughter
"I don't want to hear another peep,
I just gave you a glass of water
Now will you please go to sleep."

After a small period of silence
He heard another plaintive plea,
"Dad, I'm still very thirsty
Will you bring a drink to me?"

"If I have to come in there daughter
I will pull my parental rank,
And as a disciplining father
Your bottom I'll have to spank"

In another five more minutes
Her new request made him think,
"Dad, when you come in to spank me
Will you bring me another drink?"

THE CAPED CRUSADER

I had a comic book hero
When I was a lad of nine,
Exciting adventures were waiting
For the price of a shiny dime.

When the evil crooks appeared
You could feel the tires squeal,
As Batman rushed to meet them
In his souped up Batmobile.

Although they used their cunning
Batman, they couldn't surprise,
The Riddler and the Joker
Soon met their demise.

That waddling old Penguin
Also turned to crime,
Although the Cat woman was evil
She certainly looked divine!

Why would wealthy Bruce Wayne
Live such a double life,
When he lived in luxury
And could have a beautiful wife.

I suspect one of the reasons
He chased crooks so corruptible,
The expense of all his equipment
He charged off as tax deductible.

LIFE'S LOOKING GLASS (A SONNET)

When I look back over the fleeting years
I realize my candle of life is low,
and the lofty goals I set, it now appears
are ambitions that I will never know.
In youth I had soaring aspirations
to achieve wealth, honor and fame world wide,
to receive status and acclamation;
but failed no matter how hard I tried.

Yet, I realize there are things I can do
To be of service to God and to man,
And I should dedicate my life anew
To use all of my remaining life span,
To make the most of every day and hour
And be guided by a loftier power.

INTERVALS (BLANK VERSE)

Is there a time in life revered by you
More than any other of your life span?
A youth thinks the moment of his first kiss
supreme, and dreams of his sweetheart divine.
Then, what could outshine career or degree?.
Another event becomes sacred when
on bended knee he says, "please marry me!?"
And she says , "I will." Later in life as
he holds his first born child, he asks, "what could
be better than this moment in my life."
Years fly-fiftieth anniversary:
then he believes this moment is the best;
Repeats his vows with more love than before.
When he reaches this point in life he knows
the holiest time of all will not come

until he meets his Maker face to face
and hears, "welcome good and faithful servant."

COUNTRY BOY

Oh, fair haired country youth
With no guile, speaking truth,
Who attended country schools
Obeying teacher, following rules;
Who did his chores every day
Before going out to play.

Didn't mind the summer heat
Of dusty lanes upon his feet,
And taking genuine delight
In heavens starry, starry light.
With nature he loves to walk
Side by side and hear her talk
Of places where the air is cool
Beside a sparkling shady pool.

He knows how to place his bait
Where bigger fish lie in wait,
Saved paper and string so he might
Make and fly his own kite.
Knowing just what time is best
To see a Robin build her nest
Or where stands a hollow tree
The home of the honeybee.

He knows what time and when
To catch a fox in her den,
Always somehow seems to know
Where biggest blackberries grow!
To soon he'll grow to be a man
Enjoy life while you can,
For looking back brings much joy
Of when I was a country boy.

THE PATH OF LIFE

The young mother set out on the path of life
Knowing the journey would bring toil and strife,
Saying, "these are the years that bring many joys
Spending many hours with each of her boys.
They were so happy and life seemed pure bliss
And she asked, "what could be better than this?"

When cold nights came with dark clouds above
She sheltered her sons with a heavenly love,
For along the journey were hills tall and steep
Her message to them, 'what you sow you shall reap."
She prayed to God they would not go astray
But follow in her footsteps day after day.

Along life's journey there was evil and hate
But when they stumbled she held them straight,
Telling, "what you see on earth is just a facade
You must place your trust in the Living God.
She often retold the old, old story
At the end of the path is everlasting glory

The days, months and years flew swiftly by
At the end of her path was a gate in the sky.
The boys watched as she walked through alone
Where her life's path led to a heavenly home,
But she would still live in their memory
And they would see her again in eternity.

WHEW!

The cowhands gathered around old Joe
Who used the split rail fence for his perch,
And he began to describe in cowboy terms
His first visit to a big city church.

"When I first got to the church" said Joe
"I had to park back in a big corral,"
"Do you mean the parking lot" asked Charles
A worldly man who was Joe's pal.

"I walked up the trail to the front door,"
"You must mean the sidewalk" Charles said,
"Inside, I was met by this dressed up Dude"
"Don't you mean usher" old Charles pled.

"Well this usher leads me down the chute"
Charles said to Joe, "You must mean the aisle,"
"This dude sat me by a young lady in a stall
Saying, I'd be there for quite a while."

"You don't mean stall," corrected old Charley
"What you should have said is pew,"
Joe mused, "that lady sitting next to me
Why, she said the same thing too!"

ON GOLDEN WINGS

God gave a special gift to Bezaleel
Before it all Israel would kneel.
He hammered out of glistening gold
Angelic beings wondrous to behold,
For God would meet Israel there
Beneath these golden wings of prayer.

These golden cherubs seem to say
God hears our prayers just one way
Forged from life's blows day by day
They teach us to look up and pray
And gives thanks for all things
As our prayer ascends on Golden wings.

Paul and Silas were wrongly jailed
Bodies beaten and thoroughly flailed,
Raised up their prayers on golden wings
And praises to God they loudly sing
As they prayed on bended knee
God sent an Angel to set them free.

Is life's problems closing in on you
Get on your knees and pray it through.
You can quench the rising tide
With the Living Lord on your side,
Take him your burdens and leave them there
By soaring on Golden Wings of prayer.

MOTHER TAUGHT ME

My Mother taught me how to twist
And now my body's a physical wreck,
From trying to turn my head to see
The dirt on back of my neck.

Mother taught me to stand firm
"You won't leave until you finish
Eating every bite upon you plate
That includes your healthy spinach."

My Mother taught me not to lie
By giving me this mandate,
I've told you over a 1,000 times
Please do not exaggerate!

Mother taught me all about life
What she said I'll never doubt,
"I brought you into this world
And I can take you out."

My mother taught me about time travel
And on when and where to speak,
If you open your mouth once more
You'll be in the middle of next week.

Mom taught me all about behaving
With "excuses please don't bother,
Pick up your clothes off the floor
And quit acting like your father."

Mother taught me a new religion
It gave my heart a tug,
You had better pray my son
That it'll come out of the rug. (cont.)

She also taught me to plan ahead
On this she wouldn't relent,
You must always wear clean underwear
In case you're in an accident.

Mother taught me about appreciation
At least from her point of view,
"There are many unfortunate kids
Who don't have parents like you."

Now that I'm grown with children
I tell my daughter and her brother,
The same old valuable life lessons
I learned from dear old Mother.

A PRECIOUS MOMENT (A SONNET)

In the beginning before there was time
A beautiful domain arose into place,
Perfection bloomed in a garden sublime
A creation none dare harm or efface.

Two earthly people were created pure
To walk with God in the cool of the day,
One yielded his soul to temptations lure
And pride caused Adam and Eve to go astray.

A heavenly convening at God's throne
Took place with the Son and Holy Spirit too,
To announce through the ages it would be known
The Son became a man for me and you.

He died on a tree to let men be free
To chose where they spend their eternity.

BAREFOOT IN THE COUNTRY

I want to leave the city pavement
And stroll barefoot once again,
Down a dusty country lane
And through fields of yellow grain.

I want to leave the neon signs
Walk under harvest moons,
Feel the grass between my toes
Hear the loon's mournful tunes.

I want to wade the creek once more
Feel the mud between my toes,
And sit upon it's grassy banks
As over the rocks it merrily flows.

I want to lie barefoot on my back
Watching the clouds come and go,
Perhaps one will bow low enough
Where I can touch it with my toe!

I know I cannot go back again
To once more have a childish lark,
So I will take off my city shoes
And go barefoot in the park.

WHY

I wonder why young children die
When their future looked so bright,
In the sky afar did God need a star
To brighten up His night.

Did God see me cry as I said goodby
To my child being laid to rest,
Could He but know, I lost the glow
Of the hope within my breast.

Like any man I try to understand
Why such tragedies do occur,
And seek relief for my grief
In front of a lonely sepulcher.

Then God replied, this child that died
Is a loss that's hard to bear,
I too had loss on a wooden cross
So your child could be my heir.

As these words sink in I'm free from sin
I fall upon my knees to pray,
I thank God above for a sacrificial love
That will reunite us again one day.

TRADING PLACES

I drove through a country town
And as I slowly moved along,
People stared at me through windows
While their radio blared a song.

I was envious of their happiness
Snug in their warm and cozy homes,
Whole families were together
While I must drive the road alone.

As I looked into each window
They seemed so happy without care
And I'm feeling sort of jealous
Wishing I could be in there.

As I slowly left the little village
This thought occurred to me,
Would they like to leave their burdens
And be free to drive with me.

Whatever roads you may travel
No matter how life is spent,
God's Holy Word will tell us
In all things just be content.

OLD FASHIONED FOURTH

I loved the old fashioned Fourth of July
celebrated under a hot summer's sky.
I'll relive it again before my memory fades
how the celebration started with a parade
that ended in front of the old bandstand
where Sousa's marches simply were grand.
The Mayor paid tribute to all of the brave
young men now sleeping in their grave,
Then we all picnicked until it was dark
feasting and frolicking in the big city park.
Old men pitched horseshoes, boys played ball
all ended abruptly when they heard dinner's call.
All the young ladies wore white cotton dresses
their hot curling irons made long curly tresses.
Potato salad, baked beans and fried chicken too
were all part of our firecracker menu.
We pulled our picnic tables into the shade
to eat ice cream that was home made.
When evening came there was a loud cry
as skyrockets screamed across the dark sky.
When the fireworks stopped and it was dark
young boys chased fireflies all over the park.
I love to look back in life's looking glass
and re-celebrate July Fourths of the past.

SECRET LOVE

His eyes looked deep into hers
As he strolled into the room,
She would be a beautiful bride
If only he could be the groom.

He wanted to touch her hand
And act just like a little child,
For her warm and radiant face
Made his heart beat rather wild.

His tongue was tied; he couldn't speak
If cupid could only give a shove,
But until that right moment came
She would just be his secret love.

The days and weeks flew swiftly by
And to give his sagging hope a lift,
He would take his meager earnings
And buy secret love a gift.

A bottle of lavender perfume
He handed this beautiful creature,
I hope you like it, Miss Smith
You're my favorite first grade teacher.

MIRACULOUS BIRTH

One of the great discoveries
For women across the nation,
Is a new childbirth procedure
Called invitro fertilization.

A sixty year old woman
Was filled with pride and joy,
By using this new method
She gave birth to a baby boy.

Her relatives and friends
Came from far and near,
To see this new relative
The old mother held so dear.

The asked to see the baby
That science helped create,
But the elderly mother said
To see him you'll have to wait.

The statement about waiting
Brought a round of sighs,
You can't see my baby
Until my baby cries.

Why can't we see him now
Said the relatives with a frown,
The 60 year old mother said
I forgot where I laid him down.

STARRY WINTER NIGHT

I own a painting by Jesse Barnes
An artist not well known,
But his ability to paint with light
Makes his works stand all alone.

He has an artistic reputation
And is called the painter of light,
This painting I love so dearly
Is named Winters Starry Night.

The evening sun is sinking low
Over a cloudy mountain range,
While the evening star is twinkling
In a night so vast and strange.

A little rivulet is softly flowing
Through banks of powdered snow,
Winding past a whitewashed church
Like a scene of long ago.

The evergreens are bowing low
With snow deep on each bough,
A solitary sleigh arrives at church
For someone has made a vow.

Looking farther down the valley
You'll see the headlights of a train,
I imagine someone's going home
To ease a Mother's heart of pain.

I see lights in all the windows
Of the little village down below,
And sense the warmth and comfort
Only those dwellers seem to know. (cont.)

When I gaze upon this painting
 It brings contentment to my soul,
And to this tired old aching heart
It will cheerfully console.

YOU KNOW ME (PSALM 139)

Oh Lord, you've searched and know me
Even when I sit down or to rise,
I can never flee from your spirit
Whether ocean's depths or heavens' skies.

Before I utter a spoken word
You know my each and every thought,
Your presence is ever before me
Such knowledge cannot be taught.

Should I try to escape your presence
Even in the darkness of the night,
To you there is no darkness
You are the eternal Shekinah light.

I am fearfully and wonderfully made
Knitted together in mothers womb,
I was woven in the secret place
To be born, to grow, to bloom.

How precious are your thoughts O Lord
As countless as grains of sand,
They promise you'll never leave me
For I'm in the hollow of your hand.

TRIBUTE TO THE OKLAHOMA ROSE

Oh Oklahoma Rose
Under windswept skies,
I pay you homage
For what you symbolize.

As you stand proudly
Under a Cimarron Sun,
You are a reminder
Of the 89er land run.

Your blood red colors
Remind of the severe,
Cruel march of Natives
On the Trail of Tears.

The Oklahoma Rose
Found in five varieties,
Stand for five tribes
In civilized societies.

With forty six petals
You're a special creation,
Like the Forty Sixth State
In this American Nation.

When it comes to creation
God had you in mind,
For just like Oklahoma
You're one off a kind!

PUT ON A HAPPY FACE

I'm *excited* to write a poem about *joy*
I hope my *jubilation* will not annoy
Those who don't like to *frolic* or be *gay*
And just want to be *glum* every day.

I love those who *revel* in *satisfaction*
And are *euphoric* with *positive* action
To make sure the world's full of *glee*
And *deligh*t in having a little *hilarity*.

Regale your friends with *charm* and *mirth*
And be *festive* while on this old earth,
A *cheerful* spirit is a priceless *treasure*
And a *glad* heart will bring to many *pleasure*.

Most people love *humor* and *merriment*
And with your *elation* they'll be content;
The world loves a person who's *upbeat*
And your outgoing *exuberance* is a treat.

Just be *ecstatic* and on a constant *high*
Gladness is a virtue, just give it a try,
All of thesee things will bring you *bliss*
And the world will give you, a great big kiss!

ETERNAL LOVE

Chris and Erin, we are happy for you
The hand of God has brought you together,
And two become one when you say "I do"
A bond that is meant to last forever.

A wedding vow is a most solemn thing
When "for better or worse," is spoken,
Words that are sealed with the gift of a ring
Promises made, never to be broken.

A Christian home can be a success
When Christ is invited to enter,
And your marriage can be wonderfully blest
With Christ Jesus in the center.

Today the sky is clear and cloudless,
Yet someday the bright clouds may fold,
And when the storms of life bring distress
That's when a Godly love takes hold.

Someday, when God blesses you with children,
They will think you are wondrously wise,
When you demonstrate true love again
Showing how to be Godly husbands and wives.

As the years pass and your hair turns grey
You'll have fond memories to treasure,
You will hold your sweetheart's hand and say
"You have blessed my life beyond measure."

When one crosses over God's crystal sea
The other will thank Him in heaven above,
Knowing your beloved is waiting for thee
To continue in eternity, your Godly love.

MY AMERICAN HOME

What does America mean to me?
A country where the world can see,
We are the nation of what's just and true
The home of the old Red, White and Blue.

On Memorial Day we honor soldiers brave
And place Old Glory on their grave,
For their sacrifice we must not betray
When we celebrate Independence Day.

In America every one has a voice
In electing leaders of their choice,
And the rule of law is for every man
A part of the Founding Fathers' plan.

Here we worship God as we choose
And have freedom to watch daily news,
And children can choose their own career
And walk in neighborhoods without fear.

We can choose who will be our friend
Or just what church we will attend,
To be in a land where I can live free
That's what America means to me.

ROADS (A HAIBUN)

The pot-holed blacktop abruptly ended with a narrow,
rutted gravel road continuing. Not enough use to justify
maintenance. Although I slow the vehicle down to
thirty, I still cringe at the pinging sound of stones
hitting my new car underneath. The road now
becomes more rutted and the fields have disappeared
into the darkened woods.

Why was I returning to the old home place? Was I
encumbered with remorse for not having returned
these many years? Was it to satisfy a sentimental
remembrance from childhood? Would it even be
standing since both parents have lain in the cemetery
for a number of years? Now I wonder what drove me
to travel this distance to revisit the one place where
I harbor intoxicating memories.

The edict of the physician rose up from my
sub-conscience, your cancer is stage four.
Time is short.

Winding rutted roads
Fading words on granite slabs
Winter winds blow cold

OLD FRIENDS

Sometimes just like a bolt out of the blue
God sends us friends, loyal and true,
Others may laugh when I fail life's test
While old friends see in me, only the best.

We have known each other for many years
We have shared laughter, joy and tears,
Others may desert me when I slip and fall
My old friends just wait for me to call.

We can share memories out of the past
These are friendships that's meant to last,
We supported each other when times were rough
We found leaning on each other was enough.

The time has been passing, we're getting old
But life long friends are as pure as gold,
I pray when my life comes to an end
I will thank God for sending me dear friends.

Who helped me face life's difficult test
My old friends are the ones I love the best.

MY SPECIAL FRIEND

As I am growing older
And my life nears it's end,
I thank the Lord above
For my special friend.

Many times when together
We do not have to speak,
Knowing my every thought
But never does critique.

Sometimes we talk for hours
Of events back in the past,
Yet, we look to the future
As our love was meant to last.

When we lie down together
And turn off the light,
We often just hold hands
Late into the night.

I will love this special friend
As long as I have life,
For this very special friend
Is my soul-mate and my wife.

ANGELS

When God created the universe
With a sweep of his might hand,
To bring order to His creation
He added a heavenly angelic band.

God sent his Angels to Sodom
To punish the wickedness there,
And Gabriel was sent to Daniel
To answer his fervent prayer.

Gabriel said to the Priest Zechariah
Your world will not be the same,
Your wife Elizabeth will bear a son
And John the Baptist is his name.

Gabriel also appeared to young Mary
Saying she would be the one,
To give a miraculous birth
To God's beloved and only Son.

When Satan came and tempted Jesus
After He had fasted for forty days,
God sent ministering Angels to Him
For the Father He always obeys.

When he was hung on the cross
Suffering in agony and pain,
Ten thousand Angels were waiting
For Jesus to call their name.

He was buried in the garden tomb
Three days he lay there alone,
Until two Angels in white appeared
And they rolled away the stone.(cont.)

When Jesus ascended to heaven
The Apostles stared into the sky,
Angels said, "in like way he'll return
And his Father He will glorify."

Personally I haven't seen any Angels
For I am sure they are rare to see,
But as I look back over my life
I know Angels have watched over me.

HAIKUS

Gentle falling snow
drifting over still valleys;
while daffodils sleep.

Fireplace coals glowing
winter winds whisper outside:
the cricket sings alone.

Softly falling rain
filling all the buttercups;
a butterfly sips.

Icicles cling to eaves;
the wise ants' larder overflows
while grasshoppers die.

Hoarded in memory;
stone marker on wind swept hill;
silence eases pain.

I'M COLOR BLIND

I envision envy when I see green
And of folks who want to be seen,
Certainly I don't like the color brown
It makes me glum and feel low down.

Yellow always denotes to me
Individuals who are cowardly;
To the color orange I'm no stranger
It seems to warn of pending danger.

When I see the color of dark blue
It makes me somber, I'll bet you too,
Black for me is not a winner
It pictures a person as a sinner.

I can survive the color of lime
But makes me nauseous most of the time,
I honestly can't comprehend pink
Admittedly I don't know what I think.

I can withstand the color grey
It makes me dismal most of the day,
And sickly green is chartreuse
Of that color I have no use.

Restaurants know the color red
Stimulates hunger, you want to be fed;
My favorite colors, I think I know
I love the colors of a rainbow!

SENSE THE SEASONS

I love the changing seasons
To *feel* the *touch* of Spring;
Hear the song of a Robin
As in the nest She sings.

I *feel* the sun *caress* my face
And *inhal*e the fragrant air,
Of new mown hay in the meadow
And I forget my every care.

Fall brings a *touch* of frost
I *feel* the air turn cool,
Hear the laughter of children
As they run home from school.

Winter brings the fall of snow
I *taste* it on my tongue,
Smell the fireplace's smoke
And *hear* old carols sung.

I'm glad God gave us senses
To *smell, hear* and *touch,*
I feel He *hears* our prayers
And loves us very much.

KALEIDOSCOPIC DAY

I love to watch a deep, dark and purple night
give way to the moon, luminous
as a yellow cheese, infusing its silver rays
vibrantly on the chocolate soil.
Morning comes, the golden sun rises
with rays like the peach complexion
of a baby on the verdant hillside,
tinting leaves of lime and forest green.

Later, under an azure sky emblazoned
with chalky white clouds, I see
wheat fields gilded with a ruddy tint
and blush under the intense rays
of a summer sun.

Then twilight comes with a sinking crimson sun
illuminating the landscape,
with pigments of amber and bronze.

No gray days for me!
In twenty four hours I have seen
 a kaleidoscope of vivid and gay colors.
If I had to choose a favorite color,
I'd pick the rainbow!

OKLAHOMA TOWNS

Allen, Clayton and **Cleveland** toured Oklahoma
Going through **Covington, Piedmont** and **Texoma**.
They met **Alex** and **Laverne** down in Weleetka
And found **Ryan, Thomas** and **Norman** living in Waurika.
They noticed that **Henrietta** and **Lindsay** both had **Bowlegs**
And found **Luther** and **Marietta** in downtown **Beggs**.
Perry and **Morris** wanted to play a little bingo
And went to the **Little City** of **Tishamingo**.
At **Mountain park Helena** had a **Fairview**
While **Dewey** fished in **Stillwater,** caught quite a few.
The circus was found at **Hugo** and **Ringling**
Dustin and **Duncan** found the acts spine tingling.
Paden, Paoli and **Panama** are nice places to go
So are **Oilton, Dallas** and old Fort **El Reno**.
Wayne found **Pauls Valley** was quite **Okay**
While **Hollis** and **Idabell** visited the town of **Jay**.
Bethany motored to **Barnsdall** and to **Wynona**
Then on to **Bartlesville** and ate in **Ramona**.
To find **Pond Creek, Blair** didn't know **Howe**
But went on to **Krebs** for mighty tasty chow.
The name of **Disney** may ring your bell
But there's no **Apaches** living in **Stilwell**.
From **Miami** to **Elk City** is famous Route 66
Dewey has a museum to legendary Tom Mix.
Go down to **Broken Bow** and to **Beavers Bend**
At **Hayworth** and **Tom** is where the road will end.
Chickasha has a Christmas spectacular light show
Visit **Granite** museums at **Lawton** and **Buffalo**.
See the Indian lore at **Talequah** and **Pawnee**
On my next trip, won't you come along with me.

FIRST CHILD

After months of patiently waiting
And several hours of intense pain,
Knowing you created a new life
Brings a joy you cannot explain.

Your baby is placed on your breast
Helping to form a bond with you,
And when you nurse your little son
Every moment you bond anew!

At home you sterilize his water
And all his clothes you sanitize,
If there's an award for cleanness
You would certainly win first prize.

You sing and hum to your little son
As you give him his daily bath,
You're filled with awe and wonder
As you hear him coo and laugh.

As your little son begins to grow
You buy him educational toys,
And you play symphonic music
No loud blaring T.V. noise.

To soon he'll leave to face the world
And someday he'll take a wife,
But will still be your baby son
As long as you have life.

Looking back on the years that's flown
You now have other children too,
But the thrill of that first born
Is forever enshrined in you.

THINGS CHANGE

When I was just a teenager
It seemed everyone knows,
Coming out of the closet meant
You just hung up your clothes.

Bunnies were small rabbits
Rabbits were not German cars,
And to be really spaced out
Was taking a rocket ship to Mars.

A pot is what Mom cooked in
And coke was just a cold drink,
Grass is what you mowed
You needed a clear head to think.

Rock music was just Grandma
Singing in the old rocking chair,
Whether your clothes were really cool
No one seemed to notice or care.

Hardware meant using real tools
And software wasn't a real word,
A chip was a piece of wood
Boys with earrings were absurd.

Aids were student helpers at school
Who volunteered their skill,
All of the girls practiced abstinence
No one had heard of the pill.

Where has all the innocence gone
Our morals are in sad array,
Oh how I wish today's youth
Could live in my perfect yesterday.

SPOKEN WORDS

In your activities every day
Be very careful of what you say,
Cruel words cut to the soul;
Frivolous words take their toll.

Promised words are often broken
Slanderous words are left unspoken,
Whispered words can ruin a name
Flattering words bring undeserved fame.

Hasty words without a thought
Are words your mother never taught,
Echoing words that are not true
Will always come right back to you.

Words of warning some will not heed
When good advice is what we need,
While tender words of sympathy
Warms the hearts of you and me.

Caressing words we should impart
To those who have a broken heart,
For a loved one lying under the sod
Say a word of prayer to your God,

Who can give new life to all men
And for this blessing we say Amen!

FAMILY TREE

One of the hobbies
Of interest to me,
Tracking down ancestors
On my family tree.

Father was a carpenter
Working with his hand,
He also was a dreamer
With castles in the sand.

Grandpa was a farmer
Bent by labor and toil,
From eking out a living
From the tired old soil.

Great grandfather left home
To sail across the sea,
To make a new life
In a land that's free.

Perhaps if I go back farther
Just to have a little lark,
I'll find that Uncle Noah's
Middle name was Clark!

THE LIFE OF RILEY

The summer day was hot and lazy
When a Mother cat named Daisy
Gave birth to us kittens in the barn,
Mother told us to use our head
If we want to be adopted
We must use all out kittenish charms.

When Miss Sarah came from the city
And told her dad she wanted a kitty
I began to leap and spring into the air,
For you see I was a'looking
For someone to do my cooking
And whose bedroom I could share.

I was getting tired of eating lizards
And I don't like mouse's gizzards
I would much prefer a tuna pie,
I certainly was elated
When Miss Sarah simply stated
I'll take this one for she's very spry.

Now I'm no longer sad and lonely
For I find that I'm the only
Pet in this large old city house,
I spend my days in keeping
Sarah happy and in sleeping
And I don't have to catch a single mouse!

YESTERYEAR

When I was a youngster
One pleasure of mine,
Was going to the movies
For just a shiny dime.

Saturday had a special
To keep me coming back,
To see who untied my heroine
From the railroad track.

I cheered in the Westerns
When upon the scene,
Rode some of my favorites
Roy, Dale and Gene.

For another Saturday special
I always got there early,
To laugh at the stooges
Larry, Moe and Curly.

And there were cartoons
That brought down the house,
The animated antics
Of Minnie and Mickey Mouse.

With World War II raging
Movietone news let us know,
We would be the victors
With our hero, G.I. Joe.

I seldom go to movies now
Most aren't fit to see,
I just stay home and watch
Old movies on T.V.

NEVER TOUCH THE STUFF

The preacher and the business man
Had lunch fifty miles from town,
The business man told the preacher
Alcohol helps make the food go down.

The preacher said he didn't drink
But said with a wistful sigh,
Since I'm fifty miles from town
I'd like to try a mar ten i.

The business man called the waitress
And the preacher said he'd try,
A drink he always wanted
He thinks it's called mar ten i.

The waitress told the bartender
This man can't pronounce his drink,
He's calling it a mar ten i,
But he said it with a wink.

The bartender told the waitress
For him to drink is sin,
For I see the old preacher man
Is right back here again.

HAVE A HEART

Valentine's day is not just for hearts
To be sent to those that are apart,
Or sent to those who live quite near
Whose love you hold, to you so dear.

It's not just for children in first grade
From construction paper, they're home made,
Or for husbands who live in mortal fear
They'll forget flowers once a year.

Valentine's day should show a love
That is Godly, sent from above,
Giving a helping hand each new day
And leading children in the right way.

A love for the family that is so strong
It's not afraid to say, sorry, I was wrong,
Valentine's day is about your daily grind
How you treat others, are you kind.

You can be a Valentine every day
By showing love in what you say,
This love can last all life through
If what you promise, you will do.

ONLY IN AMERICA

Only in America
There is a good chance,
A pizza will come faster
Than an ambulance.

There is another situation
That makes me stop and think,
Why is there handicap parking
In front of the skating rink?

Ordering double cheeseburgers
And fries seem like a joke,
When we think we are healthy
By insisting on diet coke.

Sitting out in the driveway
Is certainly no mirage,
It's a thirty thousand auto
While junks sits in the garage.

Drug stores make the sick
Walk all the way to the back,
While the healthy buy cigarettes
Right off the front door rack.

Both bank doors are open wide
To allow me to withdraw some tens,
But chained to their counter
Are their cheap and flimsy pens.

At that same modern bank
There's another new detail,
All the ATM machines
Have inscriptions in Braille.(cont.)

With all this modernization
I just say gol dern ya,
Trying to figure it all out
Gives me a mental hernia!

THE HIGH COST OF LIVING

The senator took a stroll
And made a wrong turn instead,
In the seedy side of Washington
A gun was placed to his head.

Senator, give me all of your money
Don't try any funny games,
With one false move from you
And I'll blow out all your brains.

The senator made no motion
The robber again made it plain,
If you don't give me your money
I'll have to blow out your brain.

The senator said to the robber
I'm not trying to be funny,
You can live here without brains
But not without your money!

SPIRIT FILLED PREACHER

There was a Baptist preacher
By the name of Brother Andy,
His only sin of commission
Was sipping on Peach Brandy.

The Deacons knew of his habit
And just to have a little fun,
Said, "we'd like to make a gift
Of Peach Brandy or Peach Rum."

They added one requirement
Just to give him a little fit,
You must thank the Deacons
From your Sunday pulpit.

Sunday he thanked the Deacons
Saying they are generously driven,
Thanks for the gift of fruit
And the spirit in which it's given.

SKINNYDIPPING

When my brother and I finished work
And sweat from our nose was dripping,
We'd wander down to the swimming hole
Where the boys went skinnydipping.

We'd find a bush or a tree nearby
On which we could hang our clothes,
And strolled along the muddy bank
Where it oozed up between our toes.

The water was green and murky
So we would never dare to dive,
But it really cooled our bodies
And made our spirits come alive..

Today's pools are full of chemicals
And I really do not enjoy
Swimming in the modern pools
As skinnydipping as a boy.

CHRISTIANS DON'T DIE

Christians don't die
They just fall asleep,
Trusting the Savior
Their soul to keep.

One glorious sunrise
A trumpet will sound,
And those sleeping
Rise from the ground.

Their spirits will join
Their bodies in air,
As their immortal soul
Was under God's care.

They did not die
A new body will form,
As they journey upward
That glorious morn.

At our Saviors feet
They will bow down,
Receiving their reward
A heavenly crown.

DOGGONE SPOILED

One of my regular routines
You can be assuming,
This spoiled pet of mine
Gets regular grooming.

I bring home little tidbits
Making sure she's always fed,
I even went out shopping
To buy her a comfy bed.

On a methodical basis
Nails are polished and clipped,
And once a year we see
That no tooth is ever chipped.

This bossy pet of mine
Is like a Russian czar,
Insists I take her riding
In our brand new family car.

A little trip in the car
Is part of my sneaky plot,
To make sure she gets
Her annual medical shot.

When dinner time is over
And I want to take a nap,
This loveable little creature
just sits down in my lap.

To beg for little treats
Which adds to my strife,
The pet gets what she wants
For she's my doggone wife!

HOLY FRIDAY

Friday is a Holy day
Her ritual will never stop,
Making the weekly pilgrimage
To the local beauty shop.

Ice storms will not prevent
Her hair from being teased,
And when she gets a perm
My bank account is squeezed.

Every six weeks or so
Janice waves her magic wand,
And lo, those old dark roots
Are turned into ashen blonde.

One Friday she was very ill
"Lets go to the doctor, my hon"
She said, "That's out of the question
Not until my hair is done.

She just prepaid her funeral
I almost blew my gasket,
Learning she had bought a mirror
To be placed inside her casket!

A DRUNK'S PRAYER

The doorbell rang loudly at three A.M.
After a car drove into their bush,
A drunk was ringing their doorbell
Yelling "please mister, I need a push."

The homeowner said to the drunk
"It's three o'clock in the morning,
I'm not going out in the rain
And please let this be a warning."

He slammed the door on the drunk
And wearily returned to his bed,
"Did you promise to help the man"
Here is what the little wife said.

"Remember when our car broke down
And in desperate need of repair,
A stranger appeared, driving us home
He certainly answered our prayer.

He wearily arose and got dressed
And went out in the pounding rain,
Yelling, "do you still need a push"
Though thinking he must be insane.

The drunk hollers from the darkness
"You sir, are treating me like a king,
I still need you to push me
I'm sitting over here in the swing!"

WHO ARE YOU?

A shoeless lad looked in the window
Of a shoe store in the city,
No one seemed to notice him
And no one showed him pity.

His clothes were torn tattered
Most likely hand me downs,
His little heart was aching
For that pair of Buster Browns.

A kind faced woman from nowhere
Came taking him by the hand,
She marched him inside the store
And to the clerk made this demand.

"Warm up a pan of water now"
Then she washed the youngster's feet,
They were black and grimy
From treading on the street.

She paid for Buster Browns
Added six pair of socks,
Promptly placed them on his feet
While he stood there in shock.

The little guy was overcome
Now that his feet were shod,
Through joyful tears he finally asked
"Are you the wife of God?"

WHICH IS PEACE

Two artists were commissioned
To paint a portrait of peace,
One started with a blue sky
With clouds like fluffy fleece.

He added a little placid lake
With a young lad in a boat,
Floating with the lazy current
In a setting serene - remote.

There were no winds to disturb
The surface of the lake,
In the quietness of the moment
You couldn't hear the Aspens quake.

The other artist began his canvas
With a raging waterfall,
And winds whipping up a spray
That reminds of a sudden squall.

On a branch above the torrent
A solitary bird has built her nest,
And sits peacefully on her eggs
With a heart that is at rest.

She knows she's safe from predators
Protected by the swirling falls,
There is peace within her breast
As to her mate she calls.

I think real peace will come when
We remain calm in facing danger,
And place our trust in the Holy Child
Born in a starlight manger.

THE CURSE OF LITTLE SALLY

Five year old little Sally
Was a most precocious child,
But the salty words she used
Would just drive her mother wild.

She was a strong willed child
And to make the matter worse,
When something went awry
She mouthed out a little curse.

Mother wanted Sally to be polite
And never gave up hope,
Saying, "if you repeat that word
I'll wash your mouth with soap.

Sally smiled sweetly at her Mother
"This is what I have to say,
If any soap touches my lips
I will certainly run away."

When her little dolls arm broke
It was the same old song and verses,
Sally blurted out loud another
One of her famous curses.

Mother took Sally by the ear
To make her regret her little slips,
Taking a bar of wet soap
And placed it between her lips.

Sally frowned at her Mother
Then shed a wistful tear,
Saying, "I'll pack my little bag
And run miles away from here."(cont.)

Mother helped pack her little bag
And pushed her out the door,
And watched Sally sit on the curb
Wondering what else lay in store.

After 30 long minutes of waiting
Mother had to make her day,
By strolling out to the curb asking
"I thought you were running away?"

Sally said sweetly to her Mother
"There's something you don't know,
I would be running away if
I knew where in the hell to go!"

WHAT THE DOG SAID

The sign on the front yard fence
Read, talking dog for sale,
A passerby wondered it it's true
Or just another con artist's tale.

He walks around to the back yard
And a black mutt is sitting there,
He asks, "are you the talking dog?"
"Yep, said the dog with a flair."

Then "what's your story" asks the man
and the Mutt looked up and said,
"I discovered my gift pretty early
And joined the CIA to get ahead."

I jetted from country to country
Sitting in rooms with diplomats and spies,
They didn't know I was listening
Which led to their demise.

But jetting the world wore me out
And I was getting somewhat older,
So I eavesdropped at the airport
And became a loyal American Soldier.

I was given a lot of plaques and medals
And a wife I also acquired;
We had several litters of puppies
And now I am just retired."

The buyer is getting excited
Asking the owner what is his price,
The owner said, "ten dollars"
He was making a sacrifice. (Cont.)

"This dog is really amazing
Why are you selling him so cheap,
If I had a dog like him
That little dog I would keep."

The dog's owner replied to the buyer
"The dog thinks he's mean and gruff,
But the dog is such a liar
He's never done any of that stuff."

A VANISHING BREED

An old west cowboy rides the fence line alone
In a frayed leather saddle as his only home,
Wearing a sweat stained hat battered from wear
That covers a head of matted, grey hair.

Searing winds have made his face wrinkled and red
His body aches from using the ground as his bed,
His visage shows the results of nature's backlash
While tobacco stains his greying mustache.

Worn leather gloves covers the burns on his hand
From using hot irons with the Lazy J brand;
A long ugly scar shows beneath his left ear
Where he was severely gored bulldogging a steer.

He doesn't mind the trail dust and all of the dirt
that's settled on the collar of his blue denim shirt,
Around his neck he wears a new red bandanna
Acquired on his last cattle drive up to Montana.

When skies darken and a thunder clouds claps
His jeans are kept dry by his brown leather chaps,
His custom made boots have worn mighty thin
And those rusty old spurs will no longer spin. (Cont.)

As he dismounts we see his right leg is lame
From being given a wild stallion to tame,
When darkness creeps in he's ready to retire
And bed himself down by the flickering campfire.

With skillet in hand over the campfire he leans
To warm up a tin can of sourdough and beans,
Before the hot coals he will kneel down or squat
To put coffee grounds in a smoke blackened pot.

In his youth he dreamed of a spread of his own
That dream vanished with the wild oats he has sown,
He knows of river crossings and a long cattle drive
From the dangers he's faced, he's lucky he's alive.

When the grim reaper comes, even cowboys must die
Pray he'll ride the fence line on that ranch in the sky.

THE DIESELFITTER

There are many strange occupations
Mine is the strangest of them all,
And I only work at it apart time
Down at the ladies lingerie mall.

I find a large pair of unmentionables
Made by an overzealous knitter,
Holding them up to the sales clerk
I say, "I tink dieselfitter".

POETIC AMBITIONS

To be a poet of renown
Is a fantasy that comes to me,
Having my words live eternal
And command immortality

I would delve for imagery
No poet had penned before,
And have readers think my poetry
Exceeds the bards of yore.

Creating a realm of mirth and whimsey
Filling each heart with delight,
Or spellbinding with a tragedy
As deep as darkest night.

I would use tinkling onomatopoeias
And repeat my alliterations,
Writing lines with internal rhymes
Is part of my aspirations.

To be revered like the old masters
Imparting precepts like they taught,
And use vivid imaginations
No other poet had thought.

And now I lay my pen down
With these dreams bold and true,
Have I found poetic success
Dear reader, it's up to you!

DOUG AND ASHLEY

Marriage is a commitment that two people make to bring out the best in each other. Happiness in marriage is not something that happens when the last "I do" is said. A good marriage is created over the years by never stopping the holding of hands and saying; "I love you" once a day.

A wife and husband are to be each others best friends and never go to sleep angry with each other, or taking the other for granted. Marriage speaks of appreciation of each other and demonstrates gratitude in many ways.

A happy marriage does not look for perfection in each other but understands and forgives mistakes that we ultimately make in life. A happy marriage cultivates being patient, flexible, understanding, and having a good sense of humor.

A happy marriage forms a circle of love with the whole family by doing things for each other out of love and not in the duty of sacrifice. It is not marrying the right partner but becoming the right partner.

As the years pass there may come a day when one of you is heartbroken or seriously ill. A happy marriage will cause the love of one to tenderly care for the other as a mother cares for a sick child.

A happy marriage is like a triangle with each of you on the bottom corners and God at the top. The closer you get to God, the closer you become to each other. With God at the center of your home there is the assurance that death will never seperate you and your love will live eternally.

WHERE I AM

When I am laid to rest
do not return to my grave
for I will not be there.

Look for me in a grandchild's smile,
the first snow of winter,
or a October harvest moon
glistening on multicolored leaves.

Find me with yellow finches at the feeder
or watching perennials pushing up through
the crusted earth. Look for me in a trellis
of red climbing roses or in picture albums
of family roots and grandchildren.

Read with me old poetry books,
 marked Bible margins
and red underlined study books.
Watch for me in fading color slides
and home movies, on old sales plaques
 and in unfinished crossword puzzles.

Walk with me in misty spring rains,
laugh with me at funny stories and hopefully
find me living in my family's heart.

ABOUT THE AUTHOR

Clark Elliott was born in 1931 in rural Kentucky and in his first book, "Reflections of My Heart" he writes about growing up in the country, his family and does so humorously. At age 13 the family moved to St. Louis where he met his beloved Louise; his first poems were written to her.

Elliott became a Christian at age 12 and was baptized in the Ohio River. He taught Sunday School for over 40 years. Many of his poems reflect his walk with the Lord.

He has no formal training in poetry but has loved poetry since childhood. He is a member of the National Poetry Society, the Poetry Society of Oklahoma and Windmill Poets. He has won over 100 awards in many states and nationally. In 2003, he was named Poet Laureate of the Poetry Society of Oklahoma.

Elliott has three children, David, Debbie and Mark. He has four grandchildren, Chris, Ashley, Jenna and C.J. A lot of time has been spent traveling between South Dakota and Atlanta, Georgia visiting the grandchildren.

His entire career was in the Life Insurance Profession in some form of management. He acquired the CLU degree and qualified for the Million Dollar Round Table. He spent 32 years with Metropolitan Life which took him from St. Louis to New York, Tulsa and ultimately to Oklahoma City, where he took early retirement to spend 9 years with Mid-Continent Life as Vice President of Marketing.

As you read this book I think you will enjoy not only the wide variety of poetry but will appreciate his great sense of humor.